Journey With Grace

New Doesn't Mean Knew…

A 21-Day Devotional

Sherilyn Jacobs Robateau

Journey With Grace

Copyright © 2024 by Sherilyn Jacobs Robateau

All rights reserved. This book is protected by the copyright laws of United States of America. No part of this book may be reproduced, distributed, or transmitted in any form or by any means, including photocopying, recording, or other electronic or mechanical methods, without the prior written permission of the publisher. Permission will be granted upon request.

Published in Miami, Florida by Smart Write Impress, a division of New Life Publishing House.

This title may be purchased in bulk for educational, business, fundraising, or promotional purposes. For more information, please email admin@newlifepublishinghouse.life.

Scripture quotations are from:

The Passion Translation® (TPT)
copyright © 2017 by BroadStreet Publishing Group, LLC.
Used by permission. All rights reserved.

The Holy Bible, New International Version (NIV)
© 1973, 1978, 1984, 2011 by Biblica, Inc.™
Used by permission. All rights reserved worldwide.

The Holy Bible, King James Version (KJV)

Holy Bible, New Living Translation (NLT)
© 1996, 2004 by Tyndale Charitable Trust.
Used by permission of Tyndale House Publishers.
All rights reserved.

SMART WRITE IMPRESS.
Miami, Florida.
https://newlifepublishinghouse.life

Cover Art by: Jaqueline Braun Loewen
Cover Design by: Loretha Green
Interior Design by: Loretha Green
Editors: Deep Read Editing Team

ISBN Paperback: 978-1-961787-08-7
ISBN eBook: 978-1-961787-09-4

Printed in the United States of America

Table of Contents

Introduction 1

New Beginnings - Day One 4

All Means All - Day Two 8

LET It Go - Day Three 12

Silence the Enemy - Day Four 16

Wait Well - Day Five 21

Trapped - Day Six 26

Never Alone - Day Seven 30

Surrender - Day Eight 35

Sweet Aroma - Day Nine 40

I Need More - Day Ten 45

WAKE Up - Day Eleven 49

Choose Life - Day Twelve 54

He Is Here - Day Thirteen 58

But God! - Day Fourteen 62

Hope - Day Fifteen 67

In Step - Day Sixteen 72

Sing, Sing, Sing - Day Eighteen 82

Weary Can Rest - Day Nineteen 87

There Remains a Rest - Day Twenty 92

Beautiful Salvation - Day Twenty-One 97

Introduction

I cannot believe it's been more than ten years! In July 2012, a part of my family, my husband, two younger, very impressionable boys, and I arrived in Puerto Rico. The boys and I had known no home other than Belize, Central America, where I was born, grew up, and met Jesus, my Savior and husband. We left behind our entire known world to discover the new that the Lord was prompting us to pursue in Him for the glory of His name.

Sure, we were all just a little apprehensive about the unknowns ahead of us, but we were also very excited that the Lord, in His awesome faithfulness, had done so much to open these doors for us. What an opportunity! We reveled in the blessings of our new home, a paradise in the Caribbean, a display of tropical beauty and possibilities.

"There was—and still is—an abundance of amazing opportunities for me to minister here, even though many oppose and stand against me." (1 Cor 16:9 TPT)

We set out to build life and ministry in Puerto Rico, as sent ones. Soon, the wind and the waves became evident, and I knew my focus, my pursuit of Jesus, our anchor and sure foundation, would be the only way for the house to stand—rather, for *me* to stand. These devotions came about in one season of determined seeking and finding Him to be my/our sustaining grace.

I promise—no, the Word of God promises that if we seek, we will find! *HE*

WILL BE FOUND. He is delighted to be found. I am glad you are taking this journey; I have prayed for you and am excited to imagine your joy in finding deeper intimacy with Jesus, the true lover of your soul.

–Sherilyn Jacobs Robateau

New Beginnings - Day One

We landed on the island just a few weeks ago and settled in an apartment. The boys are off to school, and I am alone. I feel so alone! I don't know anyone! No one to speak to, no more work, business, or ministry! What did I say yes to? I don't speak Spanish! I don't belong here! And the boys, how are they going to do this? As I walk around the community, trying to escape the four walls and quiet my thoughts, I hear the Holy Spirit whisper, "Just *be* with me. Be still and enjoy being a daughter; you don't need to do anything!" Lord, but I don't know how!

Often, we can get extremely busy doing lots of good things for the Lord: business, different ministries, service at my local church, etc. Could it be that we become dependent on these lesser sources for our soul provision, our affirmation of self-worth and purposefulness? God had so much more for us, but we must look to Him wholeheartedly. Father has good plans for us, but they are found in Him.

Like He did me, the Holy Spirit beckons you to Himself because He is what our overwhelmed soul truly needs. He is our Abba—and the root word of Abba/Father is SOURCE? Just saying!

Additionally, the Lord truly looks forward to close fellowship with you. He longs to sit with you in intimate conversation, where He unfolds the glorious plans for your life. Position yourself to receive sustenance for your spirit, soul, and body, resting assured that He is ready to supply all your needs.

Take the time today and speak openly and freely with your Heavenly Father. Dedicate yourself to Him and ask Him to encounter you daily in this journey. I encourage you to journal all the Holy Spirit reveals and speaks to you. As you seek, the Lord will make Himself found!

✝ Scripture References

Jeremiah 29:11-13 NIV

"For I know the plans I have for you," declares the Lord, "plans to prosper you and not to harm you, plans to give you hope and a future. 12 Then you will call on me and come and pray to me and I will listen to you. 13 You will seek me and find me when you seek me with all your heart."

Matthew 6:33 NIV

"But seek first his kingdom and his righteousness, and all these things will be given to you as well."

Additional Scripture:
Psalm 62

🙏**Prayer Activation**

Lord, in every beginning, you are God. Do something new in me, I pray. I ask for your grace today to partner with the Holy Spirit in discovering your mind and heart for me. Cause me to know you more, I ask in Jesus' name, Amen.

All Means All - Day Two

Moving here has stripped me of everything I have confidently known: comforts and cheerleaders! I am agitated with this stillness, this nothingness, this unfamiliar, uncomfortable place. I am slowly grasping that God called me to become the sacrifice, a LIVING SACRIFICE! In this new place of scary unknowns and trepidations of not belonging, I needed to stay on the altar by choice, not squirming off because of the heat, the discomfort. Lord, help me!

Have you ever been in a place where the Lord asked you to surrender all? That is where I found myself. He asked me to let my ideas, presumptions, and fears die on His altar! Holy Spirit affirmed, "Yes, I have removed all the crutches;

now lean on Me." I recalled David's account in 1 Chronicles. Everything was set, prepared by another for him to present an offering to God. How easy it would have been for him to just go ahead and take that route, but David knew that wouldn't do! He understood that a sacrificial offering was his own heart being presented on that altar. Hence, David determined that he must bear the cost. He paid the total price! I, too, was on the altar. As I surrendered, my offering was soaked with many tears, releasing fears, loneliness, inadequacies, and more. He was making room for new things, beyond my imagination, that He had in store for me.

Friends, remember, God wants everything! He is ultimately after wholly devoted hearts expressed in totally surrendered lives. What is the Lord asking you to sacrifice today to go deeper with Him? Getting up earlier, fasting food, entertainment, etc., may be just the very start. Ask Him! And settle in your heart to pay FULL PRICE, give it all, because He is worth it! He is with you and is eager to lead you into His greatness.

Go forth today in the joy of the Lord and great expectations of Him! He is Good!

✝ *Scripture References*

Psalm 118: 27-28 TPT

"For the Lord our God has brought us his glory-light. I offer him my life in joyous sacrifice. Tied tightly to your altar, I will bring you praise. For you are the God of my life and I lift you

high, exalting you to the highest place."

Psalms 27:14 TPT

"Here's what I've learned through it all: Don't give up; don't be impatient; be entwined as one with the Lord. Be brave and courageous, and never lose hope. Yes, keep on waiting—for He will never disappoint you!"

Additional Scripture: 1 Chronicles 21:23-26

🙏Prayer Activation

Lord, thank you for paying the ultimate price on the cross for my forgiveness and new life. Lord, I belong to you, and I know your thoughts toward me are for good. God, today I ask for courage to surrender all. In Jesus' name, I pray. Amen.

LET It Go - Day Three

We cannot hold the old and new in our hands at the same time! Packing up our children and things to leave life in Belize was only the surface level of letting go and this first stage honestly was so laced with excitement and expectancy; who would have known what was to come? To my surprise, the pain of detachment eventually pressed upon me in ways I didn't anticipate, like a flood of tears in seeing the Belize flag lifted high. My heart was always to impact Belize; now, my heart was broken, and my mind was confused. In this season, the enemy vehemently attacked my soul, my mind, and my emotions! But the Lord invited me deeper into Him, calling me to give Him my cares and dreams in exchange for His, exceedingly more than I imagined.

I think God is constantly inviting His children to a Divine Exchange—what you have versus what your soul truly needs, where you are versus where He wants you to be, His invitation to trade your old for His new. The exchange He offers is freedom from hindrances and bondages to release the greatness that He brings. *James 4* shows us how. It reveals that submitting to God is preemptive to our resisting the enemy's strategies against us! As one pastor says, "When we turn on the light, roaches flee!" Walk in LIGHT because light shone forth always displaces the darkness, activating divine exchange in our lives.

Undoubtedly, the Holy Spirit is beckoning you forward, desiring to take you from strength to strength, faith to faith, and glory to glory. Pay attention to your talk, attitudes, how you prioritize time, and anything the Holy Spirit highlights. Truly, friends, submit to God and partner with the Holy Spirit to become weightless, leaving behind every hindrance. Now, we can run with Him! Run to Win!

✝ Scripture References

James 4:7 NIV

"Submit yourselves then, to God. Resist the devil and he will flee from you."

Hebrews 12:1 NKJV

"Therefore, we also, since we are surrounded by so great a cloud of witnesses, let us lay aside every weight

and the sin which so easily ensnares us and let us run with endurance the race that is set before us."

<u>*Additional Scripture: John 10:10 NKJV*</u>

> 🙏Prayer Activation
>
> Heavenly Father, I desperately need your Holy Spirit's presence and grace in my life. Let go of what feels safe and what I have known is hard, but I want more of what you have for me. Thank you for giving me the strength to trust you and let go of all You ask, in Jesus' name. Amen.

Silence the Enemy - Day Four

I am caught in stormy seas! Some days, I would feel utterly helpless, scared to drive across the five-lane highways into this wild Puerto Rican traffic. On other days, I wondered if I was invisible to the neighbors! God, why did you bring me here? Emotions were many, but JOY was running low! Of course, joy would be something worth stealing, for as it goes, so does our strength! Now, truth be told, I was never one to look weak, so I was compelled to keep up the show! My friends and family saw the pictures and knew that God had brought me here and that I was having nothing less than a fantastic time. But for how long could this charade last? God desires truth in the inner parts.

We are all running a race, but we are also in the fight of faith. Our spiritual weapons are not conventional or natural but supernatural, invisible weapons ordained by God. They are God-empowered spiritual forces, such as prayer, fasting, and the Word. One day, in a vision, I heard His challenge; I saw something lying on the chair and the Lord saying, "I gave you a weapon to fight, but you must CHOOSE to pick it up!" I knew He was referring to my praise! Sometimes, we find ourselves in storms. But we cannot allow the storms to define who God is in our lives.

Possibly, the most powerful and versatile weapon given to us is PRAISE! The garment of praise displaces heaviness and restores joy, our strength. These faith proclamations shift our perspective from the problems to the bigness of our God and enthrone the conquering lion in our midst. Hope rises as our bold declarations silence the enemy! We will often not feel like rejoicing; nevertheless, believe the Word. There is invisible spiritual power in our praise.

Join the fight, warriors. I encourage you to use the weapon of praise wherever possible: at home, in the car, or at church! Enjoy praise music, sing and dance along, play a musical instrument, or read your favorite Psalm of Praise aloud! His joy will be your strength.

It's going to be a great day!

✝ *Scripture References*

<u>***2 Corinthians 10:3-4 NKJV***</u>
"For though we walk in the flesh, we do not war according to the flesh. For

the weapons of our warfare are not carnal but mighty in God for pulling down strongholds."

<u>*2 Corinthians 2:14 NKJV*</u>

"Now thanks be to God who always leads us in triumph in Christ and through us diffuses the fragrance of His knowledge in every place."

<u>**Additional Scripture: Psalms 34:3, 8 NKJV**</u>

🙏**Prayer Activation**

Lord, thank you for the freedom to praise! I exalt you, Lord God Almighty, above all else, for you are worthy of praise. Lord, please overtake every heaviness, fear and pride in me and shift the spiritual atmosphere of my life, in Jesus' name, amen.

Wait Well - Day Five

I know my Heavenly Father had an incredible plan when He brought us to PR, and I expected it would be explosively evident. However, there I was, thrust into this uncomfortable middle, in the waiting! What was evident is that I wanted this dream to happen without fully embracing the changes that had to occur in ME and my family. I found myself fixated on the difficulties we faced, and my internal world was becoming miserable, with ugly attitudes and behavior to suit. I was not waiting well, even after seeming to surrender to the Lord. Like we often do, I sometimes got swept into grumbling, complaining, and spewing out the gloomiest expectations.

I imagine apparent needs and the looming trials in all our lives act as flashing neon signs demanding attention. We needed NOW answers that sometimes seemed so hard to come by. We may have been seeking rescue from bondages, consolation in difficult losses, wisdom and guidance in crisis, and more. Amid our sense of urgency, however, is the need to wait on God! Are we waiting well? God, in His faithfulness, will use the challenges to our comfort to build character and grow our capacity! God's Holy Spirit graciously invites us into some essential word based principles. Firstly, let our hearts be expectant of God and His goodness. He is good. Without this expectancy, we will lose heart, become faint, or even depressed. Expectancy is the breathing ground for miracles! Purposely recall His goodness to you because He doesn't waver in love and faithfulness. He will come through again. Secondly, support our waiting with rejoicing and thanksgiving! Yes, we intentionally give Him our attention because what we focus on is MAGNIFIED!

Thirdly, constrain and direct your speech to agree with God's words and your expectation of GOOD. As we behold the void, the darkness, we get to be like our Father and speak life into the circumstances. Finally, remember after we do all we know to do, silence and stillness may be the best next course to take! We can all agree that waiting is a huge challenge! But it's amazing how we get to know God better in the waiting. He comes and shows Himself strong. Additionally, while He surely gives us the peace, joy, and courage to wait, He also brings us through at the appointed time with renewed strength and faith. My friends, WE are transformed in the waiting!

✝ *Scripture References*

Philippians 4:6-7 NKJV

"Be anxious for nothing, but in everything by prayer and supplication, with thanksgiving, let your requests be made known to God; and the peace of God, which surpasses all understanding, will guard your hearts and minds through Christ Jesus."

Isaiah 40:31 NKJV

*"But those who wait on the Lord
Shall renew their strength;
They shall mount up with wings like eagles,*

*They shall run and not be weary,
They shall walk and not faint."*

Additional Scriptures:
Psalms 27:13-14 NKJV

🙏Prayer Activation

Holy Spirit, I need your strength to wait patiently and joyfully. Help me to trust you and look forward to the increased faith and strong character that you are building in me. I receive your working in me Lord, in Jesus' name. Amen.

Trapped - Day Six

The sad reality for many seasoned believers is we become stuck in the routines, the learned church jargon and the religious patterns. We need more sincerity and authenticity. That was me, complacent and confident in my dutiful obedience to God. Subtle self-righteous pride poked gaps in my spiritual wall and armor and I was unaware. I was blindsided, struggling to navigate these difficult life circumstances, health issues, and prevailing family challenges. Honestly, I was trapped within myself by unrealistic expectations of the supposedly mature Christian. And I mostly just felt alone!

The prophet Nehemiah once found Israel in a dreadful situation. The walls of Jerusalem were in shambles, leaving the city vulnerable to invasion by human enemies or beasts. He rallied the people to repair and rebuild. During the project, they faced many distractions and persecution, but he instructed them to work with one hand and carry the sword in the other, remaining sober and alert to the enemies' strategies!

We, too, have a wall of great importance to attend to; Isaiah called it the wall of salvation. This refers to our great salvation in Jesus, forgiveness of sin, reconciliation with God, our Father, for eternity, and promised abundant life with Him starting here on earth. But be aware, we also have an enemy who seeks gaps in our wall, opportunities to steal, kill, and destroy us and our family! Breaches can form in our armor and walls due to apathy in our relationship with the Lord, weakness of character, independence/pride, disobedience, and many more. We are all tasked to build and maintain our walls and guard our lives from these enemy ploys. Let's take the example from Nehemiah to be diligent in repairing the gaps in the walls that may give the enemy access to our lives and family. How do we do that? Daily wall maintenance looks like partnering with His Spirit, who is working in us to bring us the fullness of salvation. Like the Israelites, we will do the necessary work and stay alert to ward off all attempts to hinder us. Give the enemy no chance; we keep our wall in good repair!

✝ *Scripture References*

Nehemiah 4:17 NKJV

"Those who built on the wall and those who carried burdens loaded themselves so that with one hand they worked at construction and with the other held a weapon."

Isaiah 60:18b NKJV

"But you shall call your walls Salvation,
And your gates Praise."

🙏 Prayer Activation

Lord, I pray for grace to stay on the wall, to be diligent in any task set before me by the Holy Spirit and to fortify my walls! Holy Spirit, as you convict and guide, I will be quick to obey, in Jesus' name. Amen.

Never Alone - Day Seven

Isolation is a trap! Isolation, whether perceived or real, is the enemy's strategy to make you and me "easy targets." The Lord was very evident in my life. Nonetheless, feelings of rejection and abandonment weighed heavily on my soul; it was bizarre. Emotions blanket the entire landscape of life, but somehow, over four decades in, I lacked the skills to manage. This realization motivated my partnership with the Holy Spirit in finding the freedom and strength I needed to thrive. I embarked on this deep-heart excavation of past hurts, lies, fears, distrust, insecurities, and more. By God's design, the process required not just surrender to Him but also deliberate yielding to the help He sent me.

God is building a house, a people that hell cannot prevail against. This is a two-fold process. First, we as individual living stones are being shaped, formed in His hands, being fashioned to His design. It is indeed such a beautiful experience to cultivate a personal relationship with our loving Heavenly Father, the Source of all we need. I have relished the adventures of an intimate daily walk with my God with joy and excitement. My mantra has been, "...it's personal, between me and YOU, Lord."

Yet, more significant still, what God is building is His family, a unit comprising many. I started to grasp that the Lord puts the lonely in families for good reasons: we would support and build each other. As His spiritual children, we are privileged to be divinely and perfectly fitted together in His glorious house! With locked arms together, we create a place where, though the enemy schemes and attacks, he cannot prevail. The Master Builder is forging us together as His magnificent church.

Like a fire stick, as bright as we can shine on our own, we are still just a little flicker that can be quickly snuffed out. But together, we can burn a more stunning glow, a display of His splendor! Get excited about being in God's house today, about the fellowship of believers, specifically those you know He has gifted you with to support you, grow you, and form the new YOU.

Scripture References

Hebrews 10:25 NLT

"And let us not neglect our meeting together, as some people do, but encourage one another, especially now that the day of his return is drawing near."

Ephesians 4:16 TPT

"For His body has been formed in His image and is closely joined together and constantly connected as one. And every member has given divine gifts to contribute to the growth of all and as these gifts operate effectively throughout the whole body, we are built up and made perfect in love."

Additional Scriptures: 1 Peter 2:5 NKJV

> 🙏**Prayer Activation**
> Father, forgive me for not esteeming your church, your body. Forgive my selfishness, independence, and pride. You have made us one. Give me courage and sincerity in my relationships, I ask, in Jesus' name. Amen.

Surrender - Day Eight

I have realized that the enemy's end game is to derail my destiny. Satan is not just my enemy; he is God's enemy first, and God's enemy is after God's glory. God created, saved, and called me to be a nation changer for His glory! My situation blindsided me, and I was in a severe sulk, a "pity" party! In His mercy, the Lord softly whispered probing questions to my heart; "…did you give your life to me?" "…will these challenges stop you from doing my will?" His gentle, loving rebuke initiated my shift in perspective. I wanted to please my Father and bring glory to Jesus. How can I lean into Him? I needed a PIVOT.

Sometimes, in our chase after God, we encounter extreme trials and obstacles coming from varied sources: living in a sinful world, our own foolish choices, choices of others, and spiritual attacks directed against us—the enemy schemes to breathe chaos and confusion into our perception of God and ourselves amid the storm. Our attention stayed fixed on the issues, magnifying the problem and our inadequacies. Concurrently, our sense of hope diminished as God seems so far and small in comparison. For so many, this strategy is coming against you, too, to rob and derail your destiny!

But, children of God, we overcome, though we may be temporarily blindsided by the enemy's tactics. We get shaken and even stumble, but He is so faithful in bringing us into good plans for our lives. As we draw near to God and He ministers wholeness, we see again the heart of our Father for us and His world. In *Isaiah chapter 6*, Isaiah saw God and experienced His touch; he then heard the heart cry of the Father, "Who will go for Us?" We, too, will start hearing His heartbeat for souls, our families, friends, and nations. May we each respond, "Here am I, send me!" and be restored on track in His purpose.

Let's all say YES to being more intentional and persistent in sowing seeds of salvation and declaring that our God reigns! The grand result is souls to the glory of God.

✝ *Scripture References*

Psalms 126:6 NKJV

"He who continually goes forth weeping,
Bearing seed for sowing,

Shall doubtless come
again with rejoicing,
Bringing his sheaves with him."

<u>Isaiah 52:7 NKJV</u>

"How beautiful upon the mountains
Are the feet of him who brings good
news,
Who proclaims peace,
Who brings glad tidings of
good things,
Who proclaims salvation,
Who says to Zion,
"Your God reigns!"

<u>Additional Scriptures:</u>
<u>Isaiah 6:6-8 NKJV</u>

🙏 Prayer Activation

Lord, I run to You to see and encounter You as Isaiah did. I want to s ee Your heart and be fueled by Your desires for people and the nations. Spirit of God, give me the courage to give you my complete YES. In Jesus' name, I pray.

Sweet Aroma - Day Nine

When the heat is turned up—oh my—some stuff rises, shows up and out of our lives! Speech, attitudes, torments, confused feelings, and unhealthy, unwise behavior—this is where I needed help from the Lord. The dark spaces were primarily in my mind, self-loathing talk! Inevitably, this showed my inability to "show up" for my family and others around me. For far too long, I was playing the part of outward composure but without personal empowerment and freedom. Thankfully, the Lord was committed to His dream of me. He was actively intimately working out my good. My actual role was to yield, to stay close to hear His voice and not the NOISE in my head and around me.

Our very lives being lived in surrender to Christ gives off the aroma of Christ wherever we go! This is what the Lord wants to exude from us in all circumstances, not the emotional and mental space I was stepping into. Recall with me walking into a room and being captivated by the aroma of something just delicious that's cooking! The sense of smell is very effective in stirring hunger. Immediately, our interest peaks; our brain sends a message that we want to taste, and a true hunger has been awakened! In essence, God desires our lives to send an invitation to the world to come and taste His goodness. Now, isn't it amazing that spiritually, we can have this effect on those around us?

I suggest then that we have an awesome responsibility to do our best to ensure that our lives are well seasoned and flavorful with the fruit of the Spirit: love, joy, peace, longsuffering, kindness, goodness, faithfulness, and self-control. And so, our lives would exude the sweet aroma of who He is in us! Indeed, it is a sobering thought, but take heart; as we surrender, we soon realize His grace is sufficient. The Holy Spirit works in us daily to do His will so we are not left alone and powerless. Indeed, our Champion leads us to this triumph! Thank You, Lord Jesus!

✝ *Scripture References*

Phil 2:12-13 NKJV

"Therefore, my beloved, as you have always obeyed, not as in my presence only, but now much more in my absence, work out your own salvation

with fear and trembling, for it is God who works in you both to will and to do for His good pleasure."

<u>Galatians 5:22-23 NKJV</u>

"But the fruit of the Spirit is love, joy, peace, longsuffering, kindness, goodness, faithfulness, gentl eness and self-control. Against such there is no law."

<u>Additional Scriptures: 2 Corinthians 2:14-17 NLT</u>

Prayer Activation

Lord, I want to stay close to your heart, in your presence daily, hearing your leading. I pray that you grow the fruit of the Holy Spirit in me so that my life will attract others to Jesus. I ask in your name, Jesus. Amen.

I Need More - Day Ten

I am so grateful that the Lord loves me too much to leave me in my old, messy ways! But heart work is hard work; this is precisely where the Holy Spirit focused! I couldn't really appreciate that I needed any more of that sort of thing! After all, how many counseling, prayer ministry, self-development workshops, etc., haven't I done? What about the cost? People would say that I don't have it all together! Finally, yielding to many promptings from the Lord, I committed to sessions with a Christian Counselor. WOW! My Father met me in those sessions, undeniably so. I encountered love and acceptance that I thought I knew until He gave me MORE!

I truly believe God's momentum is always forward and not backward; it is always deeper, higher, and more in Him. Today, ask yourself, can I go deeper? The scriptures describe a river of God, an amazing supply of God's abundance of everything we might possibly need! It flows from the throne of God! It's the very presence of our Mighty God! In a vision, the angel of the Lord took the prophet Ezekiel into the river of God. With each step, the angel took a measurement and carried Ezekiel deeper! He was ankle-deep, knee-deep, waist-deep, and eventually, the river consumed him. Take a quick evaluation of where you are and how you are doing. No, it's not a time for guilt or self-condemn, but for pursuing more. Eternity is in Him; we will all continuously be reaching after more.

Beloveds, recommit to press in further in your times of prayer, worship, or reading His Word. Ask the Lord, in this season, what more do you ask of me? I don't know; maybe your feet are touching the water, or maybe you are quite some ways in already, but wherever you are, I know He is calling, "Come a little deeper!" Take courage and resolve to go deeper. Invite the Holy Spirit to impart the exceedingly more He has for you! Whatever you do, let's not settle in the river's shallow edge. Come on IN, the water is FINE!

✝ *Scripture References*

Psalms 46:4 NIV

***"There is a river whose streams make glad the city of God,
the holy place where the Most High dwells."***

<u>Ephesians 3:20 NLT</u>

"Now to him who is able to do immeasurably more than all we ask or imagine, according to his power that is at work within us."

<u>Additional Scriptures:</u>
<u>Ezekiel 47:1- 12, Psalm 42:7NIV</u>

Prayer Activation

Holy Spirit, I welcome you in my life. Come, Spirit of God, and reveal new things to me. Revealer of truth, show me the way to live for you, and reveal your thoughts and plans for me. I ask in Jesus' name. Amen

WAKE Up - Day Eleven

I honestly do not know where I would be if God didn't intervene in my life! Jesus rescued me from a life of aimless living at twenty years old and brought me into such a blessing. I was and am immensely grateful! The problem now is my contentment and comfort with MY blessed life! I had a nagging feeling that what Jesus purchased with His life was far beyond this. But, really I couldn't find in myself the urgency, the motivation to discover MORE. Wake up, Sherilyn, life in Christ was never meant to be just a casual walk or skipping in the park, BUT a pursuit of Him and living out destiny! The Spirit of God started to fuel my heart and passion again!

Jesus, our beautiful Savior, lived an exemplary life on earth, teaching and demonstrating the Kingdom. His appointment with the cross and triumph over the grave secured abundant life on earth and eternal life with the Father. Then Jesus returned to the Father. Now what?? Jesus ascended to Heaven and left His disciples with the same commission that He had started: to reconcile the world to the Father and establish His Kingdom on earth for the glory of God. For this reason, He then gave the Holy Spirit the Source of all we would ever need to do His will.

It is said that the Holy Spirit works in us, for us, and through us for others! Indeed, maybe we have been so selfish with the marvelous things He has done, given, and is doing in our lives. He calls us

His witnesses! Let the redeemed of the Lord say so! It is time for us to proclaim in words and deeds that the Kingdom of God is here where we are! He has good work prepared for us, even greater works than He did! This is why Jesus reassured His disciples that it was beneficial to them that He left; His ascension made the gift of His Spirit available to all who would receive Him. We need the Holy Spirit to be His witness and do His kingdom work. We can't do it in our strength and wisdom.

✝ *Scripture References*

Acts 1:4-5, 8 NKJV

"And being assembled together with them, He commanded them not to depart from Jerusalem, but to wait for the Promise of the Father, "which," He said, "You

have heard from Me; for John truly baptized with water, but you shall be baptized with the Holy Spirit not many days from now."

"But you shall receive power when the Holy Spirit has come upon you and you shall be witnesses to Me in Jerusalem and in all Judea and Samaria and to the end of the earth."

<u>*Ephesians 2:10 NLT*</u>

"For we are God's masterpiece. He has created us anew in Christ Jesus so we can do the good things he planned for us long ago."

<u>*Additional Scriptures:*</u>
<u>*John 14: 12, 16-18 NLT*</u>

🙏 **Prayer Activation**

Jesus, thank you for giving us another like You, our Helper, Holy Spirit. Holy Spirit, we need you. Empower us to know and receive ALL that Jesus accomplished on the cross, to share this gift of salvation with others, and to glorify our Father. In Jesus' name. Amen.

Choose Life - Day Twelve

Have you noticed that it's much easier to talk about (or post) all the bad or challenging things that are going on? Others are often too eager to join in to size up and compare distresses. My friends, not only is this a gloomy way to approach life, but this focus will bear only bad fruit! Now, I acknowledge the need and cathartic benefits of releasing our cares and the heavy, unrealistic burdens we carry when we try to do it alone. Oh, what needless pain we bear, all because sometimes we do not pursue Him in prayer, whether be it on our own or through agreement from a trusted prayer partner.

However, I want to counsel us that God is not impressed by our grumbling, complaining, or rehearsing of our problems to others. I remember the Lord challenging me regarding the story I am telling. I was giving the enemy too much attention. My mind needed a shift to who my God is and what He promised in His Word. Though the Lord has great compassion for His people, He is positively moved on our behalf by our faith. He has, in advance, made provision for us on a cruel cross and He wants us to acknowledge and receive what He has already paid for us to have. This is the journey of faith, growing from faith to faith. Hence, it's crucial that what we speak is faith, agreeing with God and His promises.

    I implore you with the Scripture that says life and death are in our tongues! Agreeing with the enemy in our speech will surely rob our joy and peace and cast despair on us. Faith has no room to arise in that atmosphere! Rather, what we focus on is magnified and our problems start to loom over us and even appear bigger than our Almighty God.

Friends, declare your faith today! Tell of God's faithfulness and your great hope in Him. By this, we will encourage and stir ourselves and others up in faith, and God will find us in faith when He comes. He is coming, and His reward is with Him!

✝ *Scripture References*

Hebrews 10:23-24 NKJV

"Let us hold fast the confession of our hope without wavering, for He who promised is faithful. And let us

consider one another in order to stir up love and good works."

Proverbs 18:21 NKJV

*"Death and life are in the power of the tongue
And those who love it will eat its fruit."*

Additional Scriptures: Luke 18:7-8 NKJV

🙏 Prayer Activation

Lord God, forgive us for our grumbling, complaining, criticism and wherever our speech has not agreed with your promises. Please speak to us your Word so that we can boldly confess our faith and expectation in you. In Jesus' name. Amen.

He Is Here - Day Thirteen

Yes, we are diligently seeking more of God's presence and power in our lives, and I believe He who hears from Heaven is always faithful and will show Himself strength! But today, I know He is here now, the God who sees and is worthy of my praise. Jesus already came and found me when I was lost in my sin. He took up residence in my heart and will never leave me nor forsake me. He is already here! I could sense His sweet, enveloping presence as the brilliant star in the sky this morning spoke of Him, that He is here bringing forth a morning of another kind.

The Lord promised that joy would come in the morning. A day is dawning when light overtakes the darkness that seems to engulf us in the moment.

Morning may not be six o'clock on our clock; there may not even be a sun rising in your area of the world to signal a new day has come. Nevertheless, I declare that NEW DAY breaks forth as the Lord separates light from the darkness looming over your life and circumstances. As in Genesis, the Holy Spirit is hovering until the divine moment when Jesus proclaims, "Let there be light," and behold, a new day is revealed for us!

The Lord is right where you are and guess what? We get to partner with Him in this process by using our words to displace darkness! We are like Him on earth; hence, the Scriptures caution that our word has the power of life and death. It is imperative, then, that we make our words proclamations of faith and in agreement with truth. We can use light words to invade the lack, the dysfunction, and darkness and partner with Christ in us to call into being kingdom realities that are meant to be!

Friends, our words go forth from us in many ways: spoken, written, songs, etc. Let's check on the words being released from us. Furthermore, we will intentionally pour forth light and life in every way possible. Let's praise our Awesome God in great expectation of His goodness. Your morning is coming!

✝ *Scripture References*

Psalm 57:8 NLT

"Wake up, my heart!
Wake up, O lyre and harp!
I will wake the dawn with my song."

Romans 4:17 NIV

"As it is written, "I have made you a father of many nations."[a] He is our father in the sight of God, in whom he believed—the God who gives life to the dead and calls into being things that were not."

Additional Scriptures:
Genesis 1:1-5 NLT,
Proverbs 18:21 NLT

🙏 Prayer Activation

Lord, we praise You for every good thing in our lives. We agree with your promises; you have done wonders and we believe you continue to push back the darkness. Thank you for the new day! In Jesus' name. Amen.

But God! - Day Fourteen

I have heard a statement that goes like this: do not accept pain in your life without having something to show for it. Labor pains, for instance, are designed to bring forth LIFE! Believe me when I say that my life has felt like labor lately! Maybe some of you can say the same. I have been frustrated, discouraged, heartbroken, fearful, and more. Unfortunately, that led to bad days where I reacted with unhealthy attitudes and ungodly responses to others. The enemy has messed with my health, my emotions, my relationships, and even my finances!

Have you experienced a little pain in life lately? Or maybe you have been experiencing pain for far too many years? Maybe the pain and the challenges are far more than you could have ever imagined for your life. I get it! In addition to the pain of tragedy, sickness, loss etc., we often also face other debilitating emotions in response to what we are experiencing. Loneliness, guilt, and shame are some that the enemy puts on us to keep us from rising as the overcomers we were called to be. The Lord promised that in this world of troubles, we OVERCOME because He already did it and paved the way for us too. However, in his attempt to derail us, the enemy will want to keep us overwhelmed, confused, and depressed, BUT we have a Savior!

Beloved, firstly, turn your eyes and pour out your heart to your Abba God, who is near to the brokenhearted and binds up our wounds. Secondly, call on a trusted friend or two and stay within a fellowship of believers. Isolation is a trap of the enemy. Adamantly receive strength and faith in connection and community as one way the Lord provides for you. Together, we can claim in the spirit that life comes from this pain! Thirdly, seek out and hold firm to His promises regarding your situation. The One who promised is faithful, so we can trust that the delay is not denial. He will keep you waiting and soon breakthrough for you.

 Believe me, as we seek Him, our perspectives shift, and circumstances change! I release faith, hope, and endurance to possess victory today! The enemy MUST release! Indeed, we know that God is working on our behalf and we will not be put to shame.

✝ Scripture References

Psalms 126:5 NKJV

*"Those who sow in tears
Shall reap in joy."*

Isaiah 50:7 NKJV

*"For the Lord God will help Me;
Therefore I will not be disgraced;
Therefore I have set My face like a flint,
And I know that I will not be ashamed."*

Revelation 5:5 NLT

"But one of the twenty-four elders said to me, "Stop weeping! Look, the Lion of the tribe of Judah, the heir to David's throne, has won the victory. He is worthy to open the scroll and its seven seals."

Additional Scriptures:
Hebrews 10:23 NIV

> 🙏 Prayer Activation
>
> Lord, we need your empowerment to wait, trust and praise in the waiting. We ask the Holy Spirit to give us the perseverance and zeal to push on and run our race to the finish. In Jesus' name. Amen.

Hope - Day Fifteen

It is a wonderful day! Hope is alive, a joyful expectation of good here in the land of the living. Honestly, I know that difficulties and painful realities push fiercely against our hope. I vividly recall the day I crawled up onto the sofa, tears flowing and in intense brokenness, feelings of failure, guilt, and hopelessness. There have been a few days like that. Ongoing conversations with doctors, counselors, and even well-meaning friends and family were unable to break through the gloominess in my heart and mind. This is where the God of all hope intervened.

The Scriptures say that hope deferred makes the heart sick! Desperately waiting for change while time ticks away and no answered prayer or conventional solution materializes makes the heartbroken and ill. Disappointment is an actual ailment of the soul that the enemy exploits in his schemes to entrap and derail the destiny of God's people. What can we do when we feel powerless to do anything? In those valley moments, first, I implore you not to be silent, seek the support of others in prayer and wisdom and, secondly, wholeheartedly cry out to the Lord in your anguish and need for Him. Believe me, He will respond in at least these two distinct ways to comfort you as He did for me.

Romans 15:13 asserts that the God of all hope supplies us with joy and peace in our beliefs so that our hope remains solid and whole. He gives peace to the mind fixed on Him and joy in our hearts that surpasses the immediate happenings. This joy is not happiness that's dependent on desirable happenings. The Holy Spirit's joy and peace are established through God's great gift of salvation; His Kingdom comes to the heart of men. This heart transformation and perspective shift, as we praise amid trials, enables us to wait in joyful expectation of a good God.

Indeed, as we determine to trust the Lord's faithful promises, the Holy Spirit comforts us in the waiting. He fortifies the soul, mind, will, and emotions in this. Then, we, too boldly echo Apostle Paul in *Romans 8* that God is working all things out for good. We know it by faith and remain hopeful until that hope is realized. Like David, we will not faint, but we will hold steadfast and see a glorious expected end.

✝ *Scripture References*

Psalms 27:13 NKJV

*"I would have lost heart, unless I had believed
That I would see the goodness of the Lord
In the land of the living."*

Proverbs 13:12 NIV

"Hope deferred makes the heart sick, but a longing fulfilled is a tree of life."

Additional Scriptures:
Romans 15:13, 8:28 NKJV

🙏 Prayer Activation

Lord, thank you for the courage to wait. We believe we will see your goodness because you are a good God and Father. You have been faithful before and you will come through again. We are waiting on You. In Jesus' name. Amen.

In Step - Day Sixteen

Joshua brought the children of Israel right up to the Jordan River. Can you imagine the excitement that must have been in the camp? However, here, with promised land in sight, Joshua and the people of God came upon a seemingly unpassable flooded Jordan River. How were they going to finally crossover? Joshua was probably feeling pretty good about how far they had come! Joshua had seen the power and faithfulness of God in his own experience as a leader and before that as he walked alongside God's servant Moses.

Furthermore, what they faced did not seem entirely new. Remember, there was a prominent Red Sea in Israel's past. Thankfully, Joshua also learned to seek

God's face at every juncture as Moses did before him. The Scriptures account how he and Israel waited on the Lord and at the appointed time, the people moved only as the ark of the covenant led them.

As we journey with God, it is essential to wait on God's leading and always keep pace with Him. Sometimes, in our great hurry, we fail to ask God where the right path is. Our knowledge or pride often causes us to assume we already know what He desires. Consider today that as we move forward, we may face seemingly familiar situations that we can be apathetic about or some unfamiliar things that challenge our hearts just a bit. Whatever the case, consider the Lord's declaration that He will do something new! He tells us as He did to Joshua: you have never been this way! The old patterns and past experiences may not fully prepare us for what's ahead. We will need to stay close to Him.

Like Joshua, let us realize that what seems familiar requires new strategies coming directly from the throne room. It is the season to walk hand in hand with Jesus, in step with Him daily in response to His leading and not leaning on our understanding. So, we remain sensitive to His voice and timing, knowing He will do amazing things among us!

✝ Scripture References

Jeremiah 6:16 NIV

"Stand at the crossroads and look;
ask for the ancient paths,
ask where the good way is, and walk in it,
and you will find rest for your souls.

But you said, 'We will not walk in it.'"

Joshua 3:1-5 NIV

"Early in the morning, Joshua and all the Israelites set out from Shittim and went to the Jordan, where they camped before crossing over. After three days the officers went throughout the camp, giving orders to the people:

"When you see the ark of the covenant of the Lord your God and the Levitical priests carrying it, you are to move out from your positions and follow it. Then you will know which way to go, since you have never been this way before. But keep a distance of about two thousand cubits[a] between you and the ark; do not go near it."

Joshua told the people, 'Consecrate yourselves, for tomorrow the Lord will do amazing things among you.'"

<u>**Additional Scriptures: Isaiah 43:18-19 NKJV**</u>

🙏 Prayer Activation

Lord, we want to be where You are. We do not want to run ahead, procrastinate and fall outside Your timing. We thank You, Holy Spirit, for being our Helper, for giving us the grace to wait and the courage to move as You lead. In Jesus' name.

Fix Your Gaze - Day Seventeen

The book of Exodus tells of the children of Israel being delivered by God out of slavery, but soon into the journey, the enemy decided to follow in pursuit! This whole drama came to a climax at the Red Sea! The armies of Egypt behind and the vast sea ahead were an overwhelmingly scary sight for the children of Israel. If ever one was "between a rock and a hard place," this was it! The truth is, though, this was yet another great and awesome opportunity for God to show Himself as their Strong Deliver, which He did marvelously!

Thinking about it, I have felt that kind of overwhelm when facing even lesser things in my journey to the promised land. I recall the Lord whispering, " The enemy makes a lot of noise, demanding attention." He then challenged me to focus my attention as the Holy Spirit showed me a vision of the enemy as an illusionist doing a show! An atmosphere is created of bright lights, smoke, elaborate costumes, gadgets, etc. The primary purpose is to distract your eyes from what is happening! These are like the enemy's darts thrown at us, ill-spoken words of others, feelings of condemnation, heartbreak, hopelessness or incessant thoughts, questions, fears, etc...

Our God is no magician. He is genuinely mighty in our midst, working all things out for good. Don't get fooled by the show that may be all around you. Fix your gaze on Jesus. The enemy only roars like a lion seeking to entrap and distract from God's present blessings and from our future hope that is steadfast, unmovable in Jesus, our Rock. Instead, I imagine the Lord astonishing us as He did with Peter and the church in Acts 12. As the church prayed, an angel of the Lord freed Peter from prison, but he was too stunned to understand what was happening. In fact, when He arrived where they were praying, the church too, at first, could not conceive that the answer was already before them! They prayed. He answered, and they were amazed, shocked! Yes, let's keep our expectations on the Lion of the tribe of Judah, who is victorious and is leading us to victory.

✝ Scripture References

Exodus 14:13-14 NIV

"Moses answered the people, 'Do not be afraid. Stand firm and you will see the deliverance the Lord will bring you today. The Egyptians you see today you will never see again. The Lord will fight for you; you need only to be still.'"

Romans 8:28 NIV

"And we know that in all things God works for the good of those who love him, who have been called according to his purpose."

Additional Scriptures:
Acts 12:1-18 NIV

🙏 Prayer Activation

Our Strong Deliverer is coming! He will come suddenly, and we will be astonished! Surprise us with your mighty presence and power, Lord. Even now, we give glory to YOU alone, who are worthy of all our praise! Hallelujah! In Jesus' name. Amen.

Sing, Sing, Sing - Day Eighteen

It's time to sing a new song! Don't get me wrong—I love me some old songs. They often refocus my heart, help recount God's faithfulness to His church, testify of ancient greats and show me His grace in my own journey. However, there is something awesome about singing a new song to the Lord; truly, the scriptures command us to do so. Singing facilitates my determination to always bless the Lord, as David commanded his soul in *Psalm 103*.

Seriously, I don't think anything else impassions my heart more than singing! Now, I am not by any means a professional, but since childhood, my depths have been provoked by music and singing. Over the years, I have found it to be a very life-transforming influence, both for the better and the worse. Music and singing impact our souls, lives and those around us. And this is why I wholeheartedly join with the Word of God and invite you to SING! This invitation is NOT just for the experts, worship leaders or star vocalists; it is for all of God's creation that He has given breath. Yes, even if you think you can't carry a note!

A new song gives voice to our hope and faith because faith comes by hearing! Our song becomes the declaration on earth of our agreement with the Lord. A new song announces the new thing that God is doing, that the new day is dawning. All this is significant as we are standing in our spiritual authority that brings His will on earth as it is in Heaven. Finally, we sing to delight in our Heavenly

Father, who is also singing over us! God Himself releases a new song in us that testifies to His dreams for us! Allow songs to flow forth from intimacy with Almighty God, who is real, present, and relevant to life in the here and NOW!

Friends, the new song is not just the new release from our favorite worship leader or group. Of course, where these songs echo your heart, do sing along. I ask, though, what's the song in your own heart? How is God unfolding in you? Sing a song, your song, to the Lord, that others will hear, fear Him, and put their trust in Him!

✝ *Scripture References*

Psalm 108 TPT

A Prayer for God's Help
A poetic psalm by King David

My heart, O God, is focused and determined.
Now I can sing my song with passionate praises!
Awake, O my soul, with the music of his splendor.
Arise, my soul, and sing his praises!
I will awaken the dawn with my worship,
greeting the daybreak with my songs of light.

<u>Zephaniah 3:17 NIV</u>
"The Lord your God is with you,
the Mighty Warrior who saves.
He will take great delight in you;
in his love he will no longer

rebuke you,

but will rejoice over you

with singing."

Additional Scriptures:

Isaiah 42:10-14

🙏 *Prayer Activation*

LORD, I will lift my song of praise to you! Holy Spirit set me free to sing and praise put a song in my heart that cannot be withheld. Let praise rise from the inside of us. In Jesus's name. Amen.

Weary Can Rest - Day Nineteen

Are you feeling a little weary today? Trust me, weariness is common to humanity. However, in this era, our need for rest is paramount, seriously going far beyond moments of fatigue since the prevalent lifestyle continuously pushes our being past reasonable limits.

Unfortunately, we do not readily recognize nor accept the extent to which this life pace is robbing wholeness from life. So, how can we stay steadfast and strong on this journey? I am happy to tell you that Jesus is the lover of your weary soul and mine. Yes, He is our soul (and sole) provider and invites us to feast from the rest He has prepared for us. We all need this provision.

Inevitably (according to my doctor), my occasional emotional/emotional overwhelm morphed into physical health issues, evidencing that I was not living above but under my circumstances. Does this sound all too familiar to you? Today, in our driven, fast-paced, excessive information and technology age, people of all ages are experiencing conditions that stem from emotional/mental overload coupled with physical exhaustion. Slowing down, holistic rest has not been people's first response in times of distress, but rather to boost our efforts in finding ways to manage it all. However, the prevalent health issues in our generation may be evidence that our lifestyle harasses the souls of mankind, hence warrants a clarion call to God's rest. The Lord entreats weary and burdened souls to cast those cares upon Him who will refresh and lighten our loads. I hear a trumpet call to REST. Can we hear it?

Friends, I encourage us to humbly offer to the Lord renewed surrender and receive grace from Him to thrive. Rest becomes our expressed decision to release control to Him and to trust Him to guide and sustain us in all things. One Bible teacher explains that Jesus gives us His easier yoke by becoming our burden bearer and sharer! First, He takes from our shoulders the responsibilities that were never ours to carry but are His to bear that are often inadvertently placed on us. Secondly, in our humble dependence, He empowers us to bear the burdens and care we are asked to carry as we journey on the earth's side. Yes, the Holy Spirit of God wants to partner with you and do the heavy lifting. Would you let Him?

Scripture References

Matthew 11:28-30 NIV

"Come to me, all you who are weary and burdened, and I will give you rest. [29] Take my yoke upon you and learn from me, for I am gentle and humble in heart and you will find rest for your souls.[30] For my yoke is easy and my burden is light."

Psalm 23:3 NIV

*"He refreshes my soul.
He guides me along the right paths for his name's sake."*

Additional Scripture:
Psalms 62:1 NIV

🙏 Prayer Activation

I give thanks to you, Lord, who gives strength to the weary. I give you my surrender today. I give my cares to you and receive your burden, which is easy in partnership with you. Lord, teach us how to enter your rest. In Jesus' name. Amen.

There Remains a Rest - Day Twenty

I don't want us to mistake rest for apathy or laziness nor misunderstand rest as a cease from doing Kingdom work. Rather, He invites us to co-labor with Him where we have been spinning wheels, falling into this same trap that can be called performance addiction or helping God. How many activities could I pack on my schedule to prove to God my commitment to Him? How often will I tell God my needs and then I am stressing to find the solutions myself? Oh, that we could be quiet within, calm, confident and resting in our Heavenly Father's care.

Rest is such a profound Truth. I am sure what I share with you here is just a glimpse! I am provoked by *Hebrews* chapter four, which proclaims that there remains a rest for the people of God as laws and the patriarchs of faith were unable to bring them into His desired rest for them. His true and complete rest is now available to us by grace through the work of the cross. However, it is more than eternal rest with God; salvation affords us rest for our bodies and souls today as we do daily life with Christ on earth. Jesus is Lord of the Sabbath, and He declares the sabbath was made for us, right?

I consider that Jesus, the Lord of the Sabbath, is increasingly unfolding Himself in this area of rest as a part of the abundant life He has come to give. Additionally, this revelation is directly linked to the momentum of the last days in both the spiritual and natural realms, where all things are moving fast and accelerating towards fulfillment of time. He has made a way for us to live triumphantly in this environment by restoring this divine order of our existence. Through a lifestyle of surrender and continuous dependence on Him as our only Source, we reinstate the life-giving flow that our spirit, soul and body were designed for.

Essentially, this divine rest involves choosing to stay yielded to His life pace in the middle of a chaotic, frantic world system by hearing and heeding His guidance to work and rest. In so doing, we step into another dimension of abiding, living in a Holy Spirit-led rhythm of grace to be productive with Him and to rest, trust and replenish Him.

✝ *Scripture References*

Psalm 62:1 NIV

"Truly my soul finds rest in God; my salvation comes from him."

Mark 2: 27-28 NIV

"Then he said to them, 'The Sabbath was made for man, not man for the Sabbath. So, the Son of Man is Lord even of the Sabbath.'"

Additional Scriptures:
Psalm 23:3, Hebrew 4:1-11 NIV

> 🙏 *Prayer Activation*
>
> *Lord, we acknowledge that our souls find rest in Christ alone! You, Jesus, are our Good Shepherd, in whom we truly lack nothing. Please help us to surrender all we can and enter your rest! In Your name, we ask, amen.*

Beautiful Salvation
- Day Twenty-One

OH! What a Good God we have, glorious Trinity: Heavenly Father who loves perfectly, Savior Jesus who came to give us abundant and eternal life and my precious Holy Spirit our help, guide and power to glorify our King of kings. This beautiful God had given such a great gift of salvation from which all our blessings and hope flow. Saints, I can testify that He redeemed my life! To live forgiven, restored to a relationship with Heavenly Father, and empowered by the Holy Spirit to serve Jesus, this is the power of God!

Recently, I had been asking God to see His power, and the Lord prompted me to appreciate that I have the greatest miracle of all: salvation. Amazingly, I started to see how every other miracle flows from salvation and leads to salvation! Yes, may I be forever grateful for the cross and saving grace? But you know what? I still desire to see more of God's manifest power in my life, family, church, and nations. Absolutely! My longing has intensified. I am drawn in by His heart's desire that many more be saved, and I am driven to pray and cry out for more of this saving miracle and other signs and wonders that point to Jesus.

Yes, may our lives reflect salvation's miracle. In His power, God is invading our lives with His marvelous divine exchange, exchanging old for the new and beauty for ashes. Let's manifest His glory like we are called to! We will not be the generation that the Scriptures warn about, a people with just the form of godliness but no power to show thereof. We do not want to be a part of that; instead, we live to be a display of His power and glory. As our lives reflect Him in this way, we are beacons that light the way for others and salt that stirs thirst for others to find Jesus, the mighty Lord, in our midst!

Friends, I leave you with this call to diligently seek the Lord and His manifest presence as we and the world so desperately need to see Jesus. Just think how a display of God's power will declare more than ever that He is real and mighty to save and confirm what a great, amazing salvation we have. We are His ambassadors!

✝ Scripture References

2 Corinthians 5:17-20 NIV

"Therefore, if anyone is in Christ, the new creation has come: The old has gone, the new is here! All this is from God, who reconciled us to himself through Christ and gave us the ministry of reconciliation: that God was reconciling the world to himself in Christ, not counting people's sins against them. And he has committed to us the message of reconciliation. We are therefore Christ's ambassadors, as though God were making his appeal through us. We implore you on Christ's behalf: Be reconciled to God."

Isaiah 61:3 NIV

"and provide for those who grieve in Zion—
to bestow on them a crown of beauty
instead of ashes,
the oil of joy
instead of mourning,
and a garment of praise
instead of a spirit of despair.
They will be called oaks of righteousness,
a planting of the Lord
for the display of his splendor."

Additional Scriptures: 2 Tim. 3:1-5 NIV

🙏 Prayer Activation

Lord, help me to represent you well, carrying your name and glory everywhere I go. And I pray many others will see your goodness in my life and call on you, Savior King. In Your name, Amen.

Closing Remarks

I thank and applaud you for joining me in exploring these past moments of my journey with grace. I am delighted to tell you the journey is endless! After passing through that intense season, today, I more confidently and joyfully traverse the hills and valleys of this life, knowing my hands are firmly held by grace. His grace is truly amazing! In those early days around which these devotions were written, the presence of the Lord, His voice, His wisdom, His discernment, His correction & redirection, His comfort, His joy, His strength & courage—they all culminated to affirm His faithful love AND that His grace (divine enablement) is sufficient for all that pertains to life now and into all the future.

Could this be the true nature of our walk with Christ as Believers?

Having been brought into His redeeming grace, He invites us to continue to walk out our magnificent salvation by grace; His very own working in us to desire and do what pleases Him (Philippians 2:12-13). This is great news! Amazing Grace! The Lord, by His Spirit, enables us to be, to do, and to receive the fullness of abundant life that He came to give. We are not left alone and to our own feeble efforts. I encourage you to purposely partner with the Holy Spirit daily for a truly blessed life. Prioritize the places of communion with the Lord and Holy Spirit; take personal time for the Word, for heart conversations with the Lord, for worship and prayer petitions. Then, make room for connection in fellowship with the body of Christ and see the life of Christ in you be multiplied by the Spirit. He is faithful and thrilled to journey with you too! In His Grace..

About the Author

Sherilyn had a personal encounter with grace at the age of 20. Since then, she has walked in awe of Him who loved her most and rescued her with a Father's love. Her heart's desire is to see women of all ages, races, and statuses discover this beautiful love and be awakened to original design and purpose. Seeing daughters of God walking in this freedom, beauty, and strength as is proclaimed in Isaiah 52:1-2 has been her focused passion for over 15 years. Sherilyn endeavors to activate women to a purpose that impacts nations through her ministry, Daughters of Zion Movement, and all her other ministry affiliations. Sherilyn is first a daughter of God and, secondly, a daughter of Belize, the Caribbean jewel in the heart of Central America. She is the proud mother of three adult sons and the honored wife of her husband, Errol, for now 27 years. Presently, Sherilyn serves along with her husband at their home church, Abundant Life Fellowship, in Puerto Rico. In addition to ministry to women, she enjoys ministering in worship, intercession, and teaching the Word. She also loves cooking up spicy Belizean dishes to share with friends.

Connect with more from Sherilyn via any of these media platforms:

❖ Email:

JWGconnect@sherilynrobateau.com

❖ FB pages:

Journey with Grace

https://www.facebook.com/journeywithgrace.org

Daughters of Zion (DOZ)

https://www.facebook.com/dozmovement

❖ Website:

www.sherilynrobateau.com

❖ YouTube:

Sherilyn Robateau

https://youtube.com/@sherilynrobateau8345

Daughters of Zion

https://youtu.be/fVJpiHwf3AM

www.ingramcontent.com/pod-product-compliance
Lightning Source LLC
Chambersburg PA
CBHW060817050426
42449CB00008B/1699